A GUIDE TO INTERNATIONAL TRAVEL

DIARY OF A TRAVELING BLACK WOMAN

TEACHING ABROAD
From Abu Dhabi to Abuja

Diary of a Traveling Black Woman: A Guide to International Travel

Mini Travel Guide Series:

Dubai, Abu Dhabi & The 5 Other Emirates You Didn't Know About...

Jamaica: Likkle, but Tallawah!

Trinidad: More Than Just Carnival...

Iceland: Nature, Nurture, & Adventure

Solo Travel: Try It At Least Once!

And more...

Diary of a Traveling Black Woman:
A Guide to International Travel

"Mini Travel Guide Series"
Volume XII - Teaching Abroad
1st Edition

Teaching Abroad
From Abu Dhabi to Abuja

Tori McNealy

The Traveling Black Women Network
Grace Royal International, LLC
Atlanta, GA

Cover Model: Tori McNealy
Cover Design: Nadine C. Duncan
Interior Design: Nadine C. Duncan

ISBN: 9798218230791
ISBN: 9798218230814 (Ebook)

Travel Guide Series, Volume XII
Printed in the United States of America

Published in the United States by:
The Traveling Black Women Network
Grace Royal International, LLC
Atlanta, GA 30316

www.travelingblackwomen.com

For my mother, Elana.
Thank you for encouraging me to move abroad and follow my dreams. And, thank you for your continued support on my journey.

And for my late father, Torriscella.
Thank you for the qualities of independence and perseverance you instilled in me. I love and miss you dearly.

Contents

Dear Black Woman,

Imagine waking up one day, selling all your belongings but packing your utmost essential items, kissing family and friends goodbye, and boarding a plane to a country you've never visited before but are about to call your new home.

In 2019, I did exactly this. I moved across the globe from Atlanta, Georgia to Abu Dhabi, United Arab Emirates. I said goodbye to teaching in the United States and entered a new era of teaching abroad internationally. Living and teaching abroad has opened the door to opportunities and experiences that I never would have imagined:

- Taking a camel ride through the vast desert sands and witnessing the **Great Pyramids of Giza in Egypt** up close--one of the oldest of the Seven Wonders of the Ancient World
- Feeling the presence of my ancestors while standing within the ancient walls of the **Elmina Castle in Ghana**--once a trading post along the transatlantic slave trade
- Venturing through the traditional souk within the **Medina of Marrakesh in Morocco,** smelling spices and gazing upon beautiful textiles
- Walking through the **cobblestone streets of Georgia,** admiring the diverse architecture and embarking on a wine and food tour consisting of tons of khachapuri and kindzmarauli

- Journeying along the **golden triangle route of India**, visiting Humayun's Tomb in Delhi, City Palace in Jaipur, and the infamous Taj Mahal in Agra
- Embarking on a summer **solo trip to Greece**, traveling through the Santorini streets, witnessing the beautiful blue domes of the three bells of Fira and the remarkable, Instagram worthy sunset in Oia
- Donning a gorgeous abaya and shayla, visiting the **Sheikh Zayed Grand Mosque**, and enjoying a traditional Ramadan iftar dinner at the Bab Al Qasr Hotel in Abu Dhabi
- Strolling through the streets of **Malta in the fall,** visiting the beautiful Barrakka Gardens and the Grandmaster Palace Courtyard in the old town of Valletta
- Spending the day at **Therme Spa in Bucharest,** soaking in the mineral pools, sweating in the sauna, and admiring the indoor botanical gardens during the springtime in Romania
- Traveling through multiple cities in **Bali, Indonesia** to visit the Lempuyang Temple, Ubud Monkey Forest, Tegallalang Rice Terrace, Sekumpul Waterfall, Gili Trawangan Island, and so much more...

I'm often asked by family and friends when I plan to repatriate back to the United States and my response is always the same. Not anytime soon. Teaching abroad has afforded me the lifestyle of my dreams. It has offered me opportunities to immerse myself within different cultures while getting to know individuals from all over the world. These experiences have broadened my mindset and improved my way of thinking.

Would I recommend others to teach abroad? Absolutely. Being an expatriate in a foreign country offers many benefits and opportunities that most people are unaware of. I'm here to share some of those benefits and opportunities with you so that you can potentially make the leap to move abroad.

In this travel guide, I will share important information about the what, why, and how regarding teaching abroad. I will also share tips for prepping and planning your move as well as my experience of teaching abroad in the Middle East (UAE) and the Motherland (Nigeria).

I hope this guide encourages you to step outside of your comfort zone and experience the world through a new lens.

Believe me, it is without a doubt worth it.

Teaching Abroad

"Teach abroad" is a term used to describe moving from your home country to another country to live and teach. There are numerous opportunities to teach abroad in a variety of settings: from private language centers such as hagwons to international educational institutions to Department of Defense or Embassy affiliated schools. Whether you're teaching English to speakers of other languages or instructing core classes to bilingual/multilingual learners, you're providing access to a quality education for children who need it.

Fun Fact:

You do not need to know or learn another language in order to qualify to teach abroad. There are numerous career opportunities at international schools all over the globe. You will most likely be teaching a diverse group of students that consist of nationals of the host country you move to and international students that have moved from other countries as well. However, keep in mind that all students' level of English fluency and proficiency will vary.

Why

The benefits of teaching abroad are unlike those in the United States. Teaching abroad allows you to inspire students, share knowledge, and immerse yourself in another culture while adapting to a new environment, and developing a broader view of the world and ultimately yourself.

Teach abroad contracts differ depending on the school and/or country you choose to work in but most usually provide the following:

- Relocation allowance
- Reimbursement for required pre-arrival medical examinations and vaccinations
- Reimbursement for excess luggage costs and/or storage of personal items
- Free accommodation either in the form of furnished housing or a housing allowance (both options may or may not include the cost of utilities and Internet)
- International health insurance including dental and eye insurance that can used in your host country and native country
- Salary in local and/or internationally recognized currency (tax free dependent upon the country)
- Retirement benefits/401K contributions
- Free tuition for dependent children (typically one to two dependents per employed staff member)
- Paid round trip flight to home of record

- Yearly professional development stipend
- Contract completion/renewal bonus

And so much more...

How

There are two options when applying for teaching abroad job positions. The first option is to apply directly. Some international schools have a careers tab on their school website in which prospective staff members can apply directly through an online portal or send their cover letter and resume to a provided email address.

The other option, which I highly recommend if you're teaching abroad for the first time, is to apply through a recruitment agency or service. There are numerous recruitment agencies available in which you can create an account online and begin applying to teaching positions abroad. Some of these recruitment agencies are free and others are available with for a specified cost for a yearly subscription. You can apply to great schools using free recruitment agencies, but keep in mind most premium international schools use paid recruitment agencies.

Here's a list of a few I recommend to get started:

Free	Paid
Teach Away	Schrole
The International Educator (TIE)	Search Associates
Global Recruitment Collaborative (GRC)	International School Services (ISS)

Most recruitment agencies offer either online or in person job fairs. In person job fairs are hosted in locations all over the world and many are hosted in several cities across the United States during the winter months, so be on the lookout. Most job fairs are offered for members of the paid recruitment agencies so keep this in mind as well. Recruitment season typically starts pretty early during the fall months of October and November for open positions for the following school year starting in August and September. This is because once you are hired and you sign a contract, it takes months to sort out background checks, visas, etc. A great way to begin is to conduct research about different international schools.

Two great websites to do this are:
- International Schools Database (free)
- International Schools Review (membership required)

There are also numerous Facebook groups specifically for Black expats working internationally. These groups are great for asking questions or using the search feature to find out useful information. The top three Facebook groups that helped me the most in my initial teach abroad job search and that I still use today are:

- Black Americans Living Abroad
- Black Americans Teaching Abroad (BATA)
- Brothas and Sistas Working at International Schools

Preparation
&
Planning

Packing

When you move abroad you will most likely downsize so you need to prioritize what to pack. The contents of what you pack will vary depending on what country you're moving to and what products are available there. A good rule of thumb is to pack at least a three to six month supply of your daily essentials or products you use consistently. That way when you move abroad, you have time to find different stores, online retailers, shipping companies, etc. that you're able to purchase your essential products from before you run out. Also, keep in mind excess baggage fees and shipping costs when you're packing. Some international schools will provide reimbursement for storage, shipping, and/or excess baggage fees upon your arrival and others do not. Read your contract carefully. Either way, you will most likely have to pay these fees up front on your own, so be sure to allocate appropriately. Those costs can add up quickly.

Your accommodation will usually have a welcome pack in it. This can include a variety of items dependent upon your school so be sure to ask for a list of provided resources in advance. This will help you know what to pack and bring with you.

When I moved abroad to the United Arab Emirates, my school covered the cost of my relocation airfare which was an economy class one-way air ticket via Etihad Airways. That ticket included one personal item, one carry on, and two checked bags.

The school also provided a one-time relocation allowance of 3,650.00 AED (about $1,000 USD at the time) upon arrival. Therefore, I had to pay a small amount out of pocket initially as I ended up bringing one additional checked bag.

When I moved abroad to Nigeria, my school also covered the cost of my relocation airfare which was an economy class one-way air ticket via Qatar Airways. That ticket included one personal item, one carry on, and two checked bags. However, they also provided up to $1,200 for storage of personal items in the home of record (paid as a reimbursement upon presentation of receipts), $2,000 for excess luggage cost of professional and personal items (also paid as a reimbursement upon presentation of receipts), and $1,000 (paid in Naira) settling-in allowance paid on arrival in cash. With these additional funds, I ended up bringing six checked bags (double what I brought my first year moving abroad).

I ended up packing differently when moving to the UAE in comparison to moving to Nigeria. This was due to the amount of items I accumulated over the three years I lived in the UAE as well as stocking up on my personal essentials. I mostly packed my favorite seasonings, toiletries, clothes/shoes, classroom decor and home decor.

In Abu Dhabi, I was provided with the following items in my furnished one bedroom accommodation upon arrival:

Bedroom	Kitchen
• 1 set of bed linen (e.g. duvet cover, 1 fitted sheet, 2 pillow cases) • 1 duvet • 2 pillows • 12 Coat Hangers	• 2 tea towels • 1 kettle • 1 toaster • 2 glasses • 2 bowls • 2 dinner plates • 2 mugs • 2 side plates • 1 set of cutlery (2 knives, 2 forks, 2 teaspoons, 2 dessert spoons)
Household/Toiletries	**Groceries**
• Dish washing liquid • Toilet rolls • Bar of soap • 1 bath towel • 2 hand towels	• 6 Bottles of water • Coffee • Milk • Sugar • Light snack (bread, butter, cheese, jam) • Biscuits • Breakfast (granola bars, orange juice)

In Abuja, I was provided with the following basic necessities in my one bedroom accommodation upon arrival:

Kitchen/Laundry	Bedroom/Bathroom
• Flatware, set of knives, plates, bowls, cups, glasses • Plastic spatula, serving spoon, slotted spoon, ladle • Set of cooking pots and a pan • Dish rack, cutting board • Microwave • Kettle • 2 kitchen sponges • Can Opener • Iron and ironing board	• 1 towel • 1 set of sheets, a blanket, two pillows • Basic cleaning supplies • Broom, mop, bucket, and dust parker • Toilet brush and holder, waste basket for each bathroom • Toilet plungers

Always be sure to check to see what type of electrical plug/voltage is used in the country you're moving to. Some of your appliances may require an adapter. Some countries have a much higher voltage than in North America and therefore many of your US appliances (such as hair dryers, straighteners, etc.) are better left at home and repurchased after you settle in your new country.

With all this in mind, I highly recommend that you make room for the following essentials that are often overlooked:

Travel Items	**Medicine**
Packing cubes	Prescription meds
Travel adapters	Birth control
Drawstring shoe bags	Vitamins
Clear toiletry bags	Cold and allergy medication
Handheld luggage scale	Anti-diarrheal medicine
External battery pack/charger	Feminine care
Extra power cords/cables	
Misc	**Home Essentials**
Insect repellent	Tension rod
Sunscreen	Shower curtain
Contact lens solution	Quality sheets/bath towels
Extra prescription contacts	Command hooks
Seasonal Essentials	**School Essentials**
Rain jacket or umbrella	Classroom decorations
	Writing tools (i.e. flair pens)

Physicals & Vaccinations

Most countries will require a pre-arrival medical check up and some may also require specific vaccinations and/or additional screening examinations. The cost of this is typically reimbursed by your school upon presentation of official receipts. Upon arrival in the United Arab Emirates, I had to pass a UAE government medical exam which included: a physical exam, blood test, chest x-ray, and full STD test panel for illnesses such as HIV and syphilis. The cost of this was covered by the school for all new employees.

Before moving to Nigeria (not upon arrival), I was also required to get a medical exam which included: physical examination, urine sample, complete blood count test, tuberculosis screening with PPD skin test, and mandatory yellow fever vaccine. My school also recommended the following vaccines before moving to Nigeria, though not required: Covid 19, Hepatitis A & B, Typhoid, Tetanus-diphtheria-pertussis, Polio (IPV 1), Meningococcal, Tuberculosis, and Haemophilus Influenza Type b (HIB). My school reimbursed the cost of these exams, tests, and immunizations up to $750.

Not only should you be sure to check with your Human Resources department about physical exams and vaccinations, but you should also check about your medical insurance coverage. Schools will typically provide medical coverage for yourself (and sometimes your spouse and dependents) within your host country as well as the country of your home of record (i.e. United States or Canada). Some schools will provide medical insurance under an international medical policy that provides for medical treatment anywhere in the world. The cost of medical insurance typically comes as a benefit within your contractual package. This cost is not deducted from your salary every month. You are however still responsible for any insurance deductibles or expenses in excess of your policy limits.

Money

Typically you do not need to exchange money to your new country's currency prior to arrival. This is because most schools will provide a cash stipend or an advance on your salary in the country's currency upon your arrival. Also, around the world there are more and more growing cashless societies. Most major US credit cards will work in countries abroad however it is best to contact your credit card provider and notify them of your move abroad so your purchases do not get flagged in their system.

Also keep in mind, depending on where you're moving to, online banking transactions from your overseas account can be difficult. Prior to relocation, contact your bank to confirm that they can accommodate banking transactions from the country you will be moving to. It would also be beneficial if you do not have one already, to consider getting a bank account designed for US citizens living abroad such as USAA or Charles Schwab. You should also consider getting a VPN prior to moving as some banking websites block activity from certain countries. I personally have a bank account with USAA and a paid annual subscription with Express VPN so that I can utilize online banking easily abroad.

And lastly, do not close your US-based accounts before moving abroad. Keep at least one open as some schools may deposit a portion of your salary into your foreign-based account. For example, in Nigeria 20% of my salary is deposited into my local GTBank account in local currency (Naira) and the other 80% of my salary is deposited into my USAA bank account in USD (a portion of this 80% is also deposited directly into my 401K account by my school).

Pro Tip: Even though you live abroad, you will still need to file taxes every year. US citizens living abroad have an automatic extension until June to file their tax return. In order to claim the foreign earned income exclusion, you must complete Form 2555. Make sure to look up the Internal Revenue Service Publication 54 Tax Guide for US Citizens and Resident Aliens Abroad for more information.

Document Checklist

Before you move to your new country, the Human Resources department at your new school will give you quite a lengthy checklist of documents that you must acquire and submit within a specified amount of time (usually within a few months turnaround).

Most schools will require the following:

- **Updated high resolution passport-size color photographs** on a white background. Bring a minimum of six to twelve additional copies in hand with you when you move – trust me, you will need them for everything.

- **Passport valid for more than 12 months.** If you need to renew your passport before applying for a visa like I had to, please plan to do so well in advance. The turn around times can be tight with governmental agencies. Not to mention, depending on where you move to, especially the Middle East, your passport must not contain stamps to specific countries.

- **Attested copies of your degrees.** Most schools do not cover the cost of attestation so make sure to budget accordingly as it can be costly. You can do the process yourself but I highly recommend paying the additional fees and using a company for the attestation process such as: Argentum, Roca, or Authenticate 4 Me. I was required to have two documents attested and paid a total of $670 for department fees, embassy fees, international mailing fees, and required Ministry of Foreign Affairs stamp. The full attestation process took about 20-30 business days to complete.

- **Background check** either in the form of a local police clearance certificate and/or an FBI identity history summary check (including fingerprints). This can be obtained in your current country or home country but you must have a record of good conduct before a visa can be issued in your name.

- Copies of your university level **transcript** (some schools request official copies only), state teaching license, and any additional education certifications that you may hold.

- **Reference letter(s)** and a verification of employment experience letter on company letterhead and signed by your current and/or most recent employer verifying dates of employment, position(s) held, and status during your tenure. Some schools may also require this document to be attested by the appropriate government department and Embassy or Consulate.

After you're able to obtain and submit all of these documents, you or your school will start the process for your work visa. This typically takes 4-6 weeks including visa stamping to passport. Depending on the country you're moving to, you may need to visit an Embassy or Consulate office in person for processing. Typically, any costs you incur for your work visa will be covered by your new school so be sure to save all receipts to submit for reimbursement.

Airport Info

Once your visa has been issued, either your school will arrange your relocation flight or you will be instructed to contact your school's travel agent to book your arrival airfare plane ticket. The cost of your ticket will be billed to the school directly. You should not have to pay for this expense out of pocket. Once you land in your host country and make it through passport control, a member of your School Leadership Team or Orientation Team will meet you at the airport upon your arrival and provide transportation to your accommodation. I'd recommend bringing a few small American bills to tip your baggage assistant and/or driver at the airport.

Staying Connected

There are two main options regarding phone service.

Option 1: You can choose to continue your US phone service (i.e. AT&T, TMobile, Verizon, etc.) and simply purchase an international plan that can be utilized abroad. If you choose this route, please research this extensively to find out the roaming costs and quality of service in the country you're moving to. You can also look into switching to Google Fi phone service for international coverage in specific destinations.

Option 2: Get a new phone service abroad in your host country. If you choose this route, my advice is to:

- Port your US phone number to a personal Google Voice account before canceling your US service phone plan
- Bring an unlocked cell phone with you to the country you are moving to

Depending on the country, you can either buy a prepaid SIM card upon arrival in the airport, visit a phone service provider store location, or wait for your residency visa to be completed and assigned a national identification number before you are able to purchase a SIM card and be assigned a local phone number.

Pro Tip: Download the mobile application Whatsapp and encourage your friends and family to do so as well. You will be able to use this app for sending texts, voice messages, location pins, making video calls (similar to FaceTime), and much more all using either WiFi or data. The app is great and an easy to use for group chats with family and friends as well.

Life in Abu Dhabi

Background

There's numerous stereotypes and misconceptions about living and working in the United Arab Emirates (UAE) that simply are not true.

Firstly, yes the United Arab Emirates is located in the Middle East but it's location does not make it an unsafe country. The United Arab Emirates is actually one of the safest countries in the world according to the Global Terrorism Index. The high level of security in the UAE directly results in the drastically low crime rate in the country. It's quite normal to leave your car or apartment door completely unlocked or purse unattended in your shopping cart while strolling the grocery store. That's just how safe the UAE is in general. Also, though Arabic is the official language of the United Arab Emirates, English is the second most common language spoken in the UAE. From road signs to restaurant menus, almost everything in the country is written in both Arabic and English. And believe it or not, the United Arab Emirates isn't as hot as you may think it is. Don't get me wrong, it is incredibly hot during the summer months, it is a desert after all. However, the weather starts cooling down around October and warming back up again as May approaches.

The UAE also isn't as conservative as many rumors say it is. The United Arab Emirates is an Islamic country with traditional values however the country is fairly tolerant and accepting of expats and foreign tourists that come from all over the world. Believe it or not, the UAE is not a dry country. Alcohol is legal to purchase and drink in licensed bars, clubs, hotels, and restaurants. Just be sure not to drink in public nor drink and drive!

FAQ:
How strict is the dress code?

Well regarding dress, it is important to take into consideration the local culture, customs, and attitudes of the local community. Working in international schools, you will be meeting parents and stakeholders from a diverse range of backgrounds. With this in mind, it is important to dress in a way that is respectful to the Muslim society in the UAE. Therefore, in business environments (i.e. schools, hospitals, government buildings, etc.), women should be covered appropriately.

As a rule of thumb, make sure:
- Skirts are loose and hang below the knee
- Blouses are loose with full coverage (no see-through material or cleavage)
- Sleeveless blouses are covered with an appropriate jacket or cardigan
- Shoulders should be covered and sleeves to just above the elbow

Remember, Abu Dhabi is a diverse city, populated by many expats and visited by tourists from all over the world. When going out during the daytime to public places where there are many locals, such as stores, cafes, parks, it is best to dress more conservatively out of respect for the host culture. However, when going out in the evenings to restaurants, lounges, and bars located within malls and hotels, it is acceptable to wear more casual clothing that may be considered revealing.

Accommodations

In the UAE, most expats live in residential compounds with other fellow expats of varying professions (i.e. teachers, nurses, military contractors, etc.). Most schools require new teachers to live within school provided housing for the first two years of their contract. School provided accommodations are typically a one, two, or three bedroom apartment depending on the size of your family (i.e. single, couple, dependents) and/or leadership ranking position (i.e. vice principal, principal, head of school). My school provided housing came completely furnished with the following:

- **Living Room:** Two piece sofa set, dining room table and four chairs, coffee table, and curtains
- **Kitchen:** Oven/stove, refrigerator, and microwave
- **Bedroom:** Bed including mattress (buy your own mattress topper), bedside tables, chest of drawers/dressing table, mirror, wardrobe, and curtains
- **Laundry:** Washing machine but no dryer (buy your own drying racks)

The residential compounds also include numerous amenities. When I lived in Abu Dhabi, I resided in the Al Rayyana Complex in Khalifa City A. The gated complex had apartments that were quite spacious, most with private balconies, built-in wardrobes, and en-suite bathrooms. If you were lucky, your apartment overlooked gorgeous views of the golf course next door at the Al Forsan Country Club. Within the complex, there was: two pharmacies, a grocery store with a cafe, two restaurants, a barbershop, a beauty salon, a nail spa, a dry cleaners, a stationary store, two gyms (one for weight lifting and one for cardio), pool, barbecue area, rooftop jacuzzi, and more. Compound living was extremely convenient!

Keep in mind that most school provided accommodations within the emirates of Abu Dhabi and Dubai do not include utilities and internet. You will need to pay for this out of your salary. For the internet, residents have the option of either Etisalat or Du as their service provider. The phone-internet bundles range in price depending on your choice of bandwidth. In terms of utilities, the Abu Dhabi Distribution Company (ADDC) will calculate your monthly electricity and water bill by reading the meter on your apartment or villa. You will receive this monthly statement either directly or from the facilities office at your school. It is your responsibility to pay on time each month as late fees will be added. If you neglect to pay your ADDC bill, they will shut your power off so make sure not to fall too behind.

Transportation

Taxi:

Taxi cabs are readily available all over Abu Dhabi at most establishments (i.e. malls, hotels, residence compounds, etc.) Public taxis are generally clean and relatively inexpensive. You simply pay what is stated on the meter. In Abu Dhabi, most taxis take cash only. In Dubai, taxis also take cards as a form of payment. You can also use ride share apps such as Uber and Careem within the UAE as well.

Renting/Buying:

Most school provided housing accommodations within the UAE are not within walking distance to your school, especially under the extremely hot weather conditions the majority of the year. Therefore, unless you want to pay to take a taxi to and from work daily, it's more cost effective to either rent or buy a car. Both options are a fairly easy process. Regarding renting, most agencies offer discounted rates for expat teachers specifically and longer-term rentals (i.e. every 10 months during the school year), so you should be able to arrange for a reasonably-priced vehicle. All of the major car rental agencies are in Abu Dhabi (Avis, Alamo, Budget, Dollar, Thrifty, Hertz, etc.). During my three years living in the UAE, I rented a small Nissan Sunny or Kia Pegas from Carfare for about $370/month. In order to rent long-term, most car rental companies will require you to have a UAE driver's license. Once you have your residency visa, you will easily be able to obtain your UAE drivers license depending on what country your original driver's license is from. You will first need to visit a hospital or clinic to get an eye exam done by an optometrist or optician. Then you will visit the Abu Dhabi Traffic Department and submit copies of the following documents: passport, residence visa/permit, current driver's license, passport photo, eye test certificate, and possibly a few other documents as well. After submitting your documents, completing the application, and paying the fee, you will receive your UAE driver's license typically on the same day.

Driving Tips:

- SALIK is an electronic toll gate system in Abu Dhabi that aims to reduce traffic congestion on key roads. If you buy a car, you should activate your SALIK account as soon as possible and attach the tag on your car's windshield. If you're renting a car, this tag will already be attached to the car's window and registered through the rental company. Every time you pass through a SALIK gate, about $1 is deducted from your SALIK account. If renting, your total charges will show on your monthly statement.
- ***Do NOT drink and drive!*** The UAE has a zero tolerance policy regarding drugs and alcohol. This is taken very seriously and the

penalties are severe. When in doubt, plan to take a taxi to and from your destination if you will be drinking any amount.

- **_Watch out for speed cameras!_** In the emirate of Abu Dhabi you can not go over the speed limit at all. In the other emirates of the UAE, you are able to go 20 KM over the speed limit. If speeding, you may or may not notice the flash from the camera, but you'll definitely know for sure if you've gotten a speeding ticket when you receive a message from the Abu Dhabi Police a few hours later.

Working

Government schools, charter schools, private schools, and international schools in the United Arab Emirates are all different. There's also schools with numerous curricula offered such as: International Baccalaureate, American, British, Canadian, French, German, Indian, etc.

I worked at GEMS American Academy in Abu Dhabi which is a for-profit international school that offers the American curriculum, Primary Years Program (PYP), and the International Baccalaureate (IB) Diploma. GEMS American Academy enrolls students starting in KG1 all the way through Grade 12. The three story school building is honestly quite massive (I got lost my first week working there) and includes a myriad of facilities to support the holistic development of students:

- 6 science labs and a makerspace classroom
- Planetarium and auditorium (that seats 500 people)
- Band, choir, and performing arts classrooms
- 2 recording studios (with green screen technology)
- 2 libraries (one for elementary and one for secondary)
- 2 full size indoor basketball courts
- Weight room, cardio room, and dance studio
- Fully equipped kitchen (for student use)
- 2 indoor swimming pools
- 4 outdoor tennis/basketball courts
- 3 playgrounds and 1 running track
- And so much more...

The school hosts tons of events throughout the school year for students and families to participate in and enjoy such as: grade level art festivals, elementary and secondary school musicals, band concerts, visual art exhibitions, weekly learning showcases, National Day celebrations, international food festivals, flag day cultural celebrations, etc. Numerous sports are offered as well at the JV and varsity level such as: swimming, volleyball, soccer, basketball, tennis, cross-country, track and field, and badminton.

On a personal note...

There will always be pros and cons to every work environment. GEMS American Academy offered me such a beneficial experience for my first teach abroad position. The biggest benefit to teaching abroad for me personally was being able to work my contract hours.

When teaching in the United States, I worked almost double my contract hours every week, going to work hours early and/or leaving work hours late, plus doing work in the evenings during the week and on my weekends.

Teaching in the United Arab Emirates I worked my contract hours only. I made it a priority to not take work home with me and because of how international schools are structured and managed, I was able to do this and still teach effectively. I had more planning time during the school week and the best part was that I had a full time education assistant (EA) in my classroom. When I taught primary grades in the United States, I didn't even have a part time teaching assistant or paraprofessional. But in the United Arab Emirates, all elementary classes have a homeroom teacher and an education assistant. This co-teaching model was a major win in my opinion.

The work week was shorter and I had more vacation/holiday time. Because the UAE is an Islamic country and the majority of staff and students at the school are Muslim, working hours are reduced during the month of Ramadan and there are vacation days for holidays such as Eid al-Fitr. The emirate of Abu Dhabi changed from a five day work week (at first Sunday through Thursday then Monday through Friday) to a four and a half day work week. Every Friday is an early release day for both students and teachers due to Friday prayer starting around 1:00 PM.

I was still required to stay after school one day per week for faculty meetings and professional development training sessions and I was also required to hold an after school activity (ASA) two quarters out of the school year, but it balanced out with less work from home hours, shorter work weeks, and more breaks throughout the school year.

Living

There are numerous grocery stores in Abu Dhabi but the two largest are LuLu Hypermarket and Carrefour. These would be most comparable to Super Walmart in the United States. There are also smaller grocery stores such as Spinneys, Waitrose, and Al Fair (formerly known as Souq Planet). Keep in mind, groceries at these stores are more expensive but they tend to offer more imported items and most locations sell pork products as well. There are special rooms within the grocery stores marked "Pork for Non-Muslims" in which you are easily able to buy pork products.

These main grocery stores offer delivery services as well for an additional cost. There is also a free grocery delivery service called Kibsons. There is no storefront as you purchase your groceries all online through the app. Kibsons offers a wide range of fresh fruits, vegetables, meat, and more that is shipped directly to your door. This was my personal go to for groceries. Online payment was easy, delivery was free, and products were high quality. You can also order takeout online from the majority of restaurants and get it delivered to your doorstep using any of the following delivery apps: Zomato, Deliveroo, or Talabat. You can pay online with a card or with cash on delivery.

Enjoying

What's there to do in the United Arab Emirates? Honestly the opportunities are endless. You're guaranteed to always find something to do in the UAE. If you enjoy shopping, you will not be disappointed by the malls in the UAE. Yas Mall, the largest in Abu Dhabi, is located on Yas Island and surrounded by several theme parks such as Warner Brothers Studios and Ferrari World. There's also The Galleria located on Reem Island that is home to several luxury brand storefronts. And then there's also Dubai Mall which is the largest mall in the world with an aquarium, ice rink, cinema, and much more.

Speaking of the largest mall in the world, the country is actually known for breaking several world records. Dubai is home to the world's tallest building, the Burj Khalifa, the world's largest Ferris wheel, Ain Dubai, and the world's deepest swimming pool, Deep Dive Dubai.

There's also the world's longest zipline in the emirate of Ras Al-Khaimah (RAK), Jebel Jais Flight, and the world's fastest roller coaster in Abu Dhabi at the Ferrari World theme park. There's actually quite a few theme parks in the UAE: IMG Worlds of Adventure, Motiongate, Legoland, Warner Bros World, Yas Waterworld, etc. The United Arab Emirates is super family friendly.

If you're looking for things to see and do in Abu Dhabi, I highly recommend:

- Visiting the Sheikh Zayed Grand Mosque
- Indulging in the 24K gold coffee at Emirates Palace
- Getting a 360° view of the city at the Observation Deck on the 74th floor of Etihad Towers
- Go kayaking and see the art exhibitions and galleries at the Louvre
- Spend ladies day at Saadiyat Beach Club with free-flowing wine and cocktails poolside
- Hop on a boat and spend the day at Zaya Nurai Island
- And so much more...

You can also drive over to the emirate of Dubai and have lunch at CÉ LA VI on the 54th floor of the Address Sky View Hotel with an amazing view of the Burj Khalifa in the background. Or, head over to Atlantis The Palm and dine at Saffron, Dubai's best party brunch (10 out of 10 recommend). Or, take a swim in the world's highest 360° infinity pool, Aura Skypool Lounge, at the Palm Jumeirah.

There's so much to see and do all over the United Arab Emirates. To keep up to date on the best restaurants, brunches, and any and all upcoming events and activities, I highly recommend checking out the Time Out Abu Dhabi and Time Out Dubai Instagram pages and websites. This is the best way to stay in the loop of everything that's going on.

Life in Abuja

Background

When I first told my family and friends I was moving to Nigeria, I was met with a lot of dissent and worry.

"Why Nigeria?"

"It's not safe there."

"You're going to be kidnapped because you're an American."

The amount of people I knew that hadn't stepped foot in the country of Nigeria but told me it was unsafe to do so was alarming. Let me be clear, when I decided to move to Nigeria there was (and still is) a travel advisory from the U.S. Department of State stating to reconsider travel to Nigeria as a direct result or the crime, terrorism, and kidnapping occurring across the country.

According to the U.S. Department of State, there was (and still is) violent crime throughout the country. Foreigners need to be aware of robbery, carjacking, kidnapping for ransom, terrorist attacks targeting schools/government buildings, etc. To be fair, Nigeria has not been the safest country that I have lived in and/or traveled to. However, I do think it is depicted as being more dangerous than what it actually is.

I live in Abuja, which is the capital of Nigeria, located in the Federal Capital Territory. This is quite central on the map of Nigeria. In Abuja, I have been able to travel alone during the day time to buy groceries, go out for lunch, get my hair and nails done, etc. without any major issues. However, I can only speak for the safety in the FCT area as I have not visited states in the North (Zamfara, Katsina, Kaduna, Kano, Bauchi, Gombe, Yobe, Borno) nor states in the South (Delta, Bayelsa, Rivers, Akwa Ibom, Cross River) as it is advised to avoid these specific areas due to civil unrest and violent crime.

Traveling around Abuja is fairly safe as long as you stay vigilant of your surroundings just like you would in any country in the world. My one key piece of advice regarding safety is to avoid traveling at night unless absolutely necessary. Whether you're traveling in a diplomatic vehicle, hiring a personal driver, or catching a shared ride (Uber/Bolt), there will be numerous police checks on the roads once the sun goes down. And to be completely transparent, these police checks are solely for extortion purposes.

If you are a dual national citizen or an expat that is perceived to be wealthy, you will be stopped. Sometimes these police checks are quick with a simple flashlight pointed into the interior of the car and a wave of the hand by the officer, indicating for the driver to move on. Or, sometimes the police checks can be longer if the officer asks the driver to pull over, turn off the engine, and force everyone to get out of the car to conduct a search of the car and the inhabitants (i.e. full pat down, bag check, etc.).

Being placed in this situation can be quite traumatizing, especially being a foreigner in a country that isn't your home. After being stopped by police numerous times, I now try to avoid staying out past

9:00 PM in the evenings for my own personal safety. I've ventured out to concerts, lounges, and parties after 9:00 PM only a handful of times and to be quite honest, it wasn't worth the risk. Again avoid at all costs if you're able to.

Another concern that my family and friends had when I informed them I had accepted a job offer in Nigeria was my health.

"Won't you get sick from mosquitoes?"

"Can't you die?"

These questions were valid but not as much of a concern as my family and friends (who again have never stepped foot in Nigeria), made it out to be. I received the Yellow Fever vaccine prior to moving to Nigeria to help prevent contracting the yellow fever virus after an infected mosquito bite. However, this was the only preventative care I chose. Some expats take prescription antimalarial drugs daily. I do not. However, I do use insect repellent when going out, especially in the evenings and during the rainy season. I have yet to contract malaria. But if I do, my school helps with early detection by providing single use testing kits in the clinic on campus. There's also a pharmacy next door within walking distance of the school compound as well as a pharmacy that delivers via WhatsApp.

Though every country has its areas of growth, Nigeria is a beautiful country with a vastly rich culture and heritage, affordable cost of living, and steadily improving infrastructure.

Accommodations

Within Abuja, most expats tend to live within company compounds or private housing complexes. These compounds and complexes are usually gated and guarded 24/7 with security. My apartment building is located on my school compound (five minute walk to work in the mornings). It has barricades, gates, barbed wire, armed officers, and security guards working 24 hours. Staff members are required to sign in and out when leaving campus. If you're entering or exiting by foot (for example to walk to the local convenience store or bush bar), you must go through a metal detector as well as have any bags you're carrying screened before being granted access to campus. If you're entering or exiting by car, security guards check underneath the vehicle in addition to the hood and trunk before being granted access to campus. The process can be time consuming but it is a necessary safety precaution.

Not only does the compound have 24-hour security, it has numerous other amenities as well. Expat staff are provided with fully furnished apartments, each with their own private balcony, stove, microwave, washing machine/dryer (two in one machine, no more need for drying racks), refrigerator, and TV. On the compound, there are: two pools, a clubhouse with a full kitchen, bar area, and BBQ grills (which can be booked for events by residents), spacious gym with cardio and weight lifting equipment, outdoor track, outdoor tennis/volleyball court, outdoor and indoor basketball courts, two soccer fields, dog park, three children's playgrounds, garden/rabbit hutch area, etc. All utilities (i.e. electricity, gas, water) within the apartment are paid for by the employer (no rent or utility bills). Teachers are also provided with Internet access on the housing compound. The connection sometimes has reliability issues, but works well for the most part. Power outages are common across Abuja, however they do not last long living on the compound as there are numerous back up generators.

When living within a compound you can also hire domestic help. The domestic help (i.e. housekeepers, nannies, dog walkers, cooks/chefs, drivers, etc.) register with security and undergo a background check and pre-employment screening process before they are able to work on the compound. If hired full time, domestic help can live in the Helper's Quarters located on the compound. This convenience is a benefit for all staff on the compound.

Transportation

Abuja has a number of taxi options available to get around. However, it is best to avoid public taxis, the green cabs and kekes (also known as tuk-tuks in other countries) as a method of transportation. Instead, it is recommended to use apps such as Uber or Bolt when getting around town. These are both safer options as drivers must register their vehicles and undergo a background check before driving for these companies.

The cost for most trips within the city is between 1,000 - 2,000 Naira (up to about $5 USD per ride). Keep in mind, it is best to use a private personal driver if you are traveling after dark. This costs more but it is worth your safety.

You can also purchase a car and drive yourself around Abuja. It is recommended to purchase a new vehicle or a slightly used vehicle from a trusted source in order to avoid any ongoing repairs as car maintenance can be a bit of a challenge. My school personally assists teachers with the process of obtaining a Nigerian driver's license, vehicle registration, and car insurance. Teachers can also apply for an interest-free loan of up to $5,000 within the initial two year contract at the school if they're interested in purchasing a vehicle. Most teachers here that have purchased vehicles have families while most single teachers tend to use Uber or Bolt to get around.

If driving without a personal driver, it's important to consider the fuel shortage in Nigeria. Price increases and labor strikes happen often and lines at gas stations can go on for several miles (people wait hours just to fill up their tank).

It's also important to consider the traffic in Abuja. Though it's nothing in comparison to the traffic in Lagos, the roads can still be quite congested during peak hours. There is a lot of aggressive driving (I've been hit riding in the backseat of a Bolt before), electrical outages on stoplights (these are rare and infrequent), and a significant lack of clearly defined lanes. I would say, use extra care and caution if you decide to drive in Abuja. I personally choose to remain a passenger princess and stick to Uber or Bolt to reach my destination.

Working

I currently work at the American International School of Abuja. It is ranked the top international school in the country. It was originally founded in 1993 but in 2006 the school moved from the Maitama area to the Durumi District of Abuja. The school is a United States Department Assisted School that is independent (not for-profit) and co-educational. The school serves students (Nigerian, American, and International) in preschool through twelfth grade. Students have the opportunity to take Advanced Placement courses in high school and graduate with a U.S. high school diploma.

Teachers work from 7:30 AM to 4:00 PM Monday through Friday. Secondary teachers are required to make themselves available for office hours at least two afternoons from 3:00 - 4:00 PM during the week. Teachers may also be required to attend meetings, workshops, professional developing training sessions, and/or other activities outside of contractual hours as deemed necessary by administrators. To be fair, this rarely occurs. This is because students have early release at 1:00 PM on Fridays and the rest of the afternoons are set aside specifically for faculty meetings, professional development sessions, etc. as scheduled by administration. If there are no meetings scheduled, teachers are able to use this time for lesson planning, grading, etc.

There are so many benefits to working at the

American International School of Abuja. Teachers are provided with $1,000 in professional development funds per school year (this price increases after the initial first year). Teachers are also offered a completion of contract payment of $2,500 per contract year worked. If a teacher is offered a renewal contract, the teacher receives a $5,000 contract renewal bonus paid with the August salary upon returning to Abuja to being the new contract.

AND, (this is my favorite part) the teacher contract also includes a Rest and Relaxation clause. Teachers are entitled to a $3,000 payment provided that they provide proof of leaving Nigeria for at least one week. The school literally pays teachers to take a vacation! It can't get much better than that.

Living

There's tons of indoor supermarkets and local outdoor markets in Abuja to shop from. However, there aren't any large stores such as a Super Walmart where you will be able to get everything you need in one place. When shopping in Abuja, be prepared to visit several stores to gather all the items on your shopping list.

I tend to buy my produce, specifically bananas and mangoes, from the vendors (aka aunties) walking up and down the street in front of the grocery store. It's a lot cheaper than buying in store, but they only take cash so make sure you're carrying some For groceries, I recommend shopping at: **4U, Delis, or Dunes**. All three of these stores have a great selection of bread, meat, cheese, and produce. They also have a variety of imported items. When you see a product, it's best to stock up on it as finding the product again can often be a hit or miss.

4U not only sells groceries but it also sells homeware, toiletries, and cleaning supplies. There is a toy store and small pharmacy on the ground floor in addition to an ice cream shop to the right of the main entrance, as well as a couple of outdoor food trucks. This is where I buy my rotisserie chicken fresh off the grill every week. They also offer delivery via OyaNow.

Delis is a relatively small grocery store that's been recently revamped to include a liquor store downstairs and a gelateria and deli section upstairs.

This is the only grocery store in Abuja where I'm able to find Ben and Jerry's ice cream. The cost of imported products is outrageously expensive ($15 for a pint of ice cream) but I splurge every now and then.

Dunes is a multi floor shopping center that contains a supermarket, bakery, delicatessen, electronics/appliance store, home furniture and goods section, pharmacy, liquor store, toy store, clothing, jewelry, and fragrance boutiques, gelateria, multiple restaurants and cafes, and so much more. If there's any one stop shop here in Abuja, it's Dunes. However, shopping here is the most expensive of them all.

If you're looking for Costco and Kirkland brand items, you can find them at stores like Exclusive and Prince Ebeano. Again, these import items are priced quite high but can be worth it. You can also find a variety of items at Jabi Lake Mall. The mall contains a Shoprite, which is a South African grocery store, in addition to several other pharmacies, clothing boutiques, beauty supply stores, and restaurants like Coldstone and Domino's Pizza.

Two outdoor markets that most people in Abuja frequent are:

Maitama Farmer's Market: This is an open air, local outdoor market that is quite clean and not super chaotic. Products can be purchased with cash or via bank transfer to vendors directly for a reasonable price.

Wuse Market: This outdoor market is extremely noisy, chaotic, and busy. I wouldn't recommend going here alone. It's better to shop here with a local Nigerian friend because you will probably receive the foreigners price when shopping alone. This is a traditional open air African market where you can purchase almost anything from meat and produce to Ankara fabric and ready-made clothing pieces to mattresses and machetes. Anything you're looking for, you can probably find here.

My school arranges transportation for teachers on Tuesday afternoons at 4:30 PM and Saturday mornings at 9:30 AM to shop at various grocery stores and markets on rotation. But for those who do not wish to leave the compound, there are several vendors that visit and sell fresh produce, meat, even homemade bagels and even tofu if you're vegan or vegetarian. Basically, there's a plug for everything.

You can also order food and alcohol for delivery using apps like OyaNow and Jumia Food. Be warned, do not order when hungry. The wait time is significantly longer than what you may be used to in western countries like the U.S. Food deliveries here typically take about 1.5 - 2 hours to receive. You can also contact restaurants directly via Whatsapp or phone call to arrange delivery as well.

The best part of living in Abuja that I find is being able to afford household help (i.e. nannies, cooks, cleaners). You can hire household help part time or full time as you need. Full time household help (5 days a week) cost less than $200 per month. I currently have a housekeeper that cleans daily (washes dishes, does laundry, etc.) and meal preps/cooks twice a week all for about $130 per month. You can not get this level of household help in the U.S. for the same price!

Enjoying

There is so much to see, do, and enjoy in Abuja. There are loads of small bush bars that sell beer, soda, and local dishes (also called small chops) such as suya, puff puff, meat pies, plantain, etc. Some even serve traditional foods such as jollof rice, stew meat, and whole roasted fish. These bush bars are usually outdoor areas with a small covering and plastic chairs and tables, nothing fancy. They make great gathering spots to watch sports games and chill after work.

If you're into physical activities, there's biking, running, and hiking clubs that you can join. There's also a golf country club in the area with 18 holes available to play through. There's places such as the Hilton Transcorp and Blue Cabana that have athletic facilities, swimming pools, and restaurants available to use and dine in at for a day pass price or membership cost.

If you're looking to shop for traditional pieces, you should check out Mama Africa Art Market. Vendors here sell a large variety of locally made crafts such as baskets, beads and jewelry pieces, wooden sculptures and cravings, paintings, Ankara outfits and accessories, etc. There's also monthly pop up shops hosted at Strobrie, a bakery and cafe with a large outdoor space. Strobrie also hosts pottery and sip and paint classes on the weekends. All events are posted on their instagram page and you can RSVP via Whatsapp. For nightlife, there's a few different options of things to do here in Abuja. If you like movies, there are three different cinemas and theaters you can visit: **Silverbird Plaza, Ceddi Plaza, and Jabi Lake Mall.**

If you like activities, you can visit **Central Park** where they offer go karting, cycling, axe throwing, paintball, mini golf, arcade games, and more. There's also the **Dome Entertainment Center** where you can go bowling, play pool or foosball, or try out some virtual reality games. If you're into live music and delicious food, I suggest checking out: **The Junkyard, Blake Resort, Jakes, or Tar-Tar.**

To stay up to date with restaurants, activities, and events happening in Abuja, I suggest following the **See Abuja** Instagram account for all the latest news in the country's capital.

On a personal note...

Living abroad outside of the United States as an expat requires a ton of patience, flexibility, and a mindset shift especially when moving to Sub-Saharan Africa.

Throughout my time living in Abuja, I've had to change my American mentality in order to adjust to the simpler way of life in West Africa. Abuja, contrary to stereotypes, is more developed than what is portrayed in the media. Yes some roads may not have traffic lights or lanes painted on the streets but it is still fairly easy to navigate around. Yes you may not be able to visit one supermarket for everything you need but you can buy things such as fresh bananas and mangoes off the street for less than $4.00. Yes Ubers and Bolts may take a bit longer to pick you up, but a 20 minute ride only costs about $2.00.

There's so many things to adjust to but also appreciate about living in Abuja. And in some ways, Abuja does in fact remind me of home in the United States. The fried chicken and red velvet waffles at Waffle Way as well as the grilled catfish at The Junkyard remind me of good ole fashioned country home cooking back home in Arkansas.

The pottery and sip and paint classes offered at Strobrie are reminiscent of the Painting with a Twist classes I would attend with girl friends for some fun. Nights out at The Council and Abbey & Pan are just like my nights out in downtown Atlanta (and yes they play hip-hop and R&B in addition to afrobeats so you know the vibes are immaculate). There's plenty to see and do in Abuja. Yes some things may be different from home but all it takes is a mindset shift and you'll be able to enjoy Nigeria all the same.

Teach Abroad Tips

Do Your Research

Before you apply and/or interview for a teach abroad job position, conduct your own research about the school(s) you're interested in.

- Look up the school on the International Schools Database and/or International Schools Review (ISR)
- Watch videos on YouTube (if available) and comb through the school's website.
- Check out the staff page to get a gauge for the diversity of educators currently employed.
- Connect with current or previous teachers that have or continue to work in your school(s) of interest via Facebook groups.

Remember to research not only the school but also what it's like to live in your prospective country of interest. Before I moved to the United Arab Emirates, I researched every detail down to where I would be able to get my acrylic nails and hair extensions done the way I wanted it (I'm very particular).

Ask Questions

When interviewing for teach abroad job positions, don't be afraid to ask questions. Sit down and make a list.

Some of the questions I always ask are:
- **What is the average length of time teachers stay at your school?** This will

give information about longevity and retention rates which is very important to consider when signing your initial two year contract and planning for the future.

- **What expectations are there for teacher participation beyond the school day?** This will indicate if you have any additional responsibilities outside your contractual hours. Remember teacher burnout is real. You want a job environment that promotes self care and teacher well being.
- **How will I be supported by senior leadership staff?** This will open up discussion about the job roles and responsibilities of instructional coaches, curriculum coordinators, etc. and also planning time in the form of department meetings, PLCs, vertical learning teams, etc.
- **What professional development opportunities are provided for educators?** This will tell you if this is a school space where you will be able to continue to grow as an educator or not.
- **How does your school promote diversity, equity, and inclusion?** This question opens the door for a more in depth conversation from the percentage of people of color employed as expat teachers to how welcoming and inclusive the campus school environment is to what (if any) DEI competence training is offered to staff members to

how represented the diverse student body is, etc.

- **Would you be able to share the current salary scale with me?**
- **Are you able to put me in touch with a member of staff who already works at the school?**

The last two questions are game changers! Typically for premium international schools, you go through at least two rounds of interviews before being offered a job position. I always ask for a salary scale and/or benefits package at the end of the first interview. Yes this is quite a direct approach but it will help you to make a more informed decision whether or not you would like to continue in the interview process or move on to other job options/opportunities you're presented with. Don't ever feel bad asking about salary. It is an important question and if a future potential employer is reluctant about sharing that information, nine times out of ten that is not the school for you.

It's also helpful in deciding if the country and school is for you by asking to speak to a current teacher at the school. Requesting to be put in contact with a current teacher is beneficial for numerous reasons. Current teachers tend to provide you with the tea to help you make a better, informed decision.

The current teacher can tell you:

- Their personal pros/cons about living in that specific country

- Their personal pros/cons about working at that specific school
- Must haves/essentials to pack when you move abroad
- And more..

Every time I've spoken to current teachers of a school prior to signing a contract, I've always been able to get an honest overview of the country and school I'm considering moving to. Teachers have been able to video conference via Zoom and provide a housing tour of the school accommodation. Teachers have sent me pictures of the classrooms and resources available/provided by the school so I had a better sense of what I was getting into. They also provided personal advice down to which dating apps to use!

Be Flexible

If this is your first time abroad, you are essentially trying to get your foot in the door. Be open to schools and countries that may not have been on your initial radar. For example, when I first began applying to teach abroad jobs, my focus was set on East and Southeast Asia. I did not consider the Middle East at all until I had schools view my ISS (International Schools Services) active account online and reach out for an interview. So keep your options open!

Notes

About the Author

My name is Tori McNealy. I am originally from Miami, Florida. I earned my Associate of Arts degree in Early Childhood Education from Broward College in 2013. I later graduated from the University of South Florida in 2015, Magna Cum Laude, with a Bachelor of Science degree in Elementary Education and ESOL Endorsement. I've also completed my Master of Science degree in Learning Design and Technology with a dual concentration in both eLearning design and development and game-based learning analytics from the University of South Florida.

I began my career as an elementary educator teaching second grade at Oak Park Elementary School in Hillsborough County, Florida. I continued on to teach third grade at Honey Creek Elementary

School in Rockdale County, Georgia. I then taught kindergarten & second grade at Kindezi at Gideons Elementary School in Atlanta, Georgia. I moved on to teach first grade at Charles Brant Chesney Elementary School in Gwinnett County, Florida.

The bulk of my teaching experience stateside has been in Title I schools working with Tier 2, Tier 3, and ESOL students. When I moved overseas to teach kindergarten, I utilized the IB Primary Years Program curriculum at GEMS American Academy in Abu Dhabi within the United Arab Emirates. After three years, I transitioned to teaching middle school students at the American International School of Abuja within Nigeria as a Design Technology Instructor.

In the future, I hope to pursue a career teaching abroad as an Innovative Learning Coach and further as the Director of Innovation and Technology at a private international school. I would also like to partner with primary and secondary education software program companies within the eLearning industry, to create supporting material and media (audio, video, simulations, role plays, games, etc.) to aid in making learning activities more engaging for all students.

I document my experience as an expat teaching abroad and traveling the world on my social media pages. Feel free to follow along on my journey and reach out if you have any questions along the way!

@taste.travel.teach

www.travelingblackwomen.com